Seasons

by Michèle Dufresne

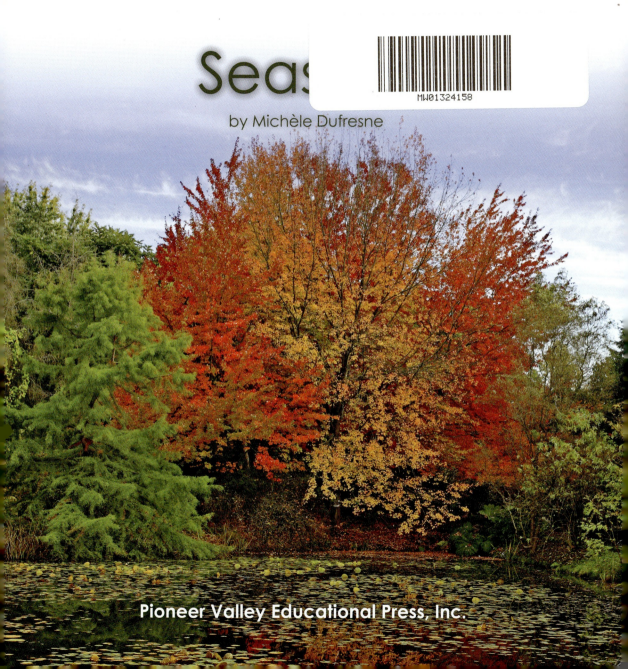

Pioneer Valley Educational Press, Inc.

In most places, the weather changes during the year. It might be hotter in the summer and colder in the winter. In the fall and spring, it might be in between. These changes in weather are called the seasons.

The seasons are different in different parts of the world. When it is winter where you live, it is summer somewhere else.

Why does the weather change?

Some people believe that
the weather changes because
the sun gets closer to the Earth
at different times of the year.
This is not true.

When it is summer where you live,
the sun shines for a longer time
each day, making the weather warmer.

When it is winter where you live,
the sun shines for a shorter time
each day, making the weather colder.

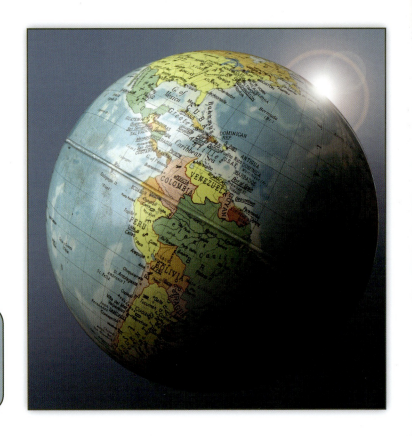

The equator is an imaginary line running around the middle of the world.

If you live near the **equator**, it will be hot most of the year. You might have only two seasons: wet and dry.

If you live near the North Pole or the South Pole, it will be cold most of the year.

Winter is the coldest season. There might be lots of snow and wind. Many animals **hibernate**.

In the spring, it begins to get warmer.

The days get longer.
Flowers begin to bloom.

Many baby animals are born in the spring.

Summer is the hottest season
of the year.

There are many colorful flowers.
You can see
birds, bees, and butterflies.

In the fall, the leaves of some trees change color.

Many birds fly to warmer places for the winter.

Some animals gather food to **store** for the winter.

Soon it will be winter.

Glossary

equator: an imaginary line around the entire world located the same distance from the north and south pole

hibernate: to rest in a sleep-like state through the winter

store: put away

Index

Fall: 2, 14
Spring: 2, 10, 11

Summer: 2, 4, 12
Winter: 2, 4, 8, 9, 14